GW00793146

To:

Clare

From:

Trevor

When your mind is
in a negative state
have a wee read.......

ISBN: 0-88396-953-x
Certain trademarks are used under license.

Manufactured in China.
First Printing: 2005

❀ This book is printed on recycled paper.

Blue Mountain Arts, Inc.
P.O. Box 4549, Boulder, Colorado 80306

Think Positive
THOUGHTS

Blue Mountain Arts®
Boulder, Colorado

May You
Always Have
Positive
Thoughts

May every day of your life bring you fresh hopes for tomorrow — because hope gives all of us our reason for trying.

May each new day bring excitement, joy, and a sense of expectation. Expect the best, and you'll get it…

May you find peace in simple things, because those are the ones that will always be there.

May you remember the good times and forget the sorrow, for the good times will remind you how special your life has been.

May you experience
all the good things in
life — the happiness of
realizing your dreams, the
joy of feeling worthwhile,
and the satisfaction of
knowing you've succeeded…

May you find warmth in others, encouraging smiles, and loyal and honest friends.

May you realize the importance of patience and accept others for what they are. With understanding and love, you'll find the good in every heart.

May you have faith in others and the ability to be vulnerable. Open your heart and really share the miracle of love and intimacy.

Above all, may you always have positive thoughts.

— Regina Hill

Motto for a
Positive
Outlook

Refuse to be unhappy;
  be cheerful instead.
Refuse to let your troubles
  multiply; just take them
  one by one…

Be optimistic.

Be energetic and positive
about the things you
do, and always hope
for the best.

Believe in yourself at all
times and in all aspects
of your life.

Before you know it,
   those wonderful dreams
   you have believed in all
   your life will come true.
   Yours will be the happy
   and successful life
   it was meant to be.

— Ben Daniels

Carry with You
These Gifts
of the Heart...

Trust...
that whatever happens,
there is someone who
will understand.

Honesty...
the feeling that you never
need to hold back...

Peace...
in being accepted for
who you really are.

Beauty...
in outlook
more than appearance.

Freedom...
to be yourself,
to change, and to grow.

Joy…

in every day,

in every memory,

and in your hopes for

the future.

Love…

to last a lifetime,

and perhaps beyond.

— D. L. Riepl

When
Difficulties
Arise...
"Hang In There"

Difficulties arise in the lives of us all. What is most important is dealing with the hard times, coping with the changes, and getting through to the other side where the sun is still shining just for you…

It takes a strong person
to deal with tough times
and difficult choices. But
you are a strong person.

It takes courage. But you
possess the inner courage
to see you through.

It takes being an active participant in your life. But you are in the driver's seat, and you can determine the direction you want tomorrow to go in…

Try not to lose sight of the one thing that is constant, beautiful, and true:

Everything will be fine — and it will turn out that way because of the special kind of person you are.

So… beginning today
and lasting a lifetime
through — hang in there,
and don't be afraid to feel
like the morning sun is
shining… just for you.

— Douglas Pagels

Positive thinking is a habit, like any other; we can practice it every day until it becomes second nature to us — and along the way, transform our lives.

— Washington L. Crowley

There is nothing either good or bad, but thinking makes it so.

— William Shakespeare

Positive Thinkers Have Twelve Qualities in Common

They have confidence in
  themselves
They have a very strong
  sense of purpose
They never have excuses
  for not doing something
They always try their
  hardest for perfection…

They never consider the
idea of failing

They work extremely hard
towards their goals

They know who they are

They understand their
weaknesses as well as
their strong points

They can accept and
benefit from criticism

They know when to defend
what they are doing
They are creative
They are not afraid to be a
little different in finding
innovative solutions
that will enable
them to achieve
their dreams

— Susan Polis Schutz

Find Something to Be Grateful for Every Day

Every day,
be full of awareness
of the beauty around you.
Be full of gratitude
for friends and family,
for the goodness you find
in others,
for your health and all
you're capable of…

Be full of acceptance
    of yourself and others —
without conditions
    or judging,
knowing that differences
and changes
    make life interesting.

Appreciate the gifts of
laughter and fun
   in your life,
and find contentment
in knowing that you
   can always control
your ability to look
on the bright side.

— Barbara Cage

Be as Happy
as You Possibly
Can Be

Love yourself every day
and remember
how many people
   love you.
Do good things
   for others, but also
give to yourself…

Release the child within you
so you can sing,
laugh, and play.
List the things
that you do best,
and give yourself a hug.

Accept compliments.

Dance barefoot.

Plan to fulfill a secret wish.

Laugh at yourself.

And above all,

remember you are loved.

— Jacqueline Schiff

You Can Make
Something Happy
Out of Everything
That Happens
in Life

Life can make choices for us. Sometimes these choices seem unhappy or unfair, but in the end we control our own destiny because we can decide how people and events affect us…

So much of our happiness

lies within

the choices we make.

We can accept that

life isn't the way

we want it to be,

or we can change it so that

it will be.

We can walk through
the shadows,
or we can choose to smile
and seek out the sunlight.
We can create grand dreams
that never leave the ground,
or we can be builders of
dreams that come true…

We can look at only
the negative aspects
of ourselves,
or we can lift ourselves up
by being our own
best friend.
We can live in the past or
dream about the future,
or we can live for today.

We can give up when the
    road becomes difficult,
or we can keep on going
until the view is much better.
The choices in life
    are endless,
and so is the potential
    for happiness.

— Nancye Sims

Make Every Day Special

Be thankful and look
to every new day
with positive hope…

Take time to pull yourself away from all the noise and just look around you. Take inventory. Appreciate those who have enhanced the quality of your life, and remember that they have been a gift to you. Also remember that you're a gift to them, too.

Be grateful for the choices you've made, both good and bad. Apply what you've learned and go on. Use these lessons to help you with your other decisions in life. Appreciate yourself and your own uniqueness...

Go outside and look at the sky. Soak in the atmosphere. Enjoy the colors of the landscape. Feel the textures of every place you are that you're thankful for. Smile at the world. Put a positive spin on every thought you have.

Make every day special.
Own it. Enjoy it. Bask in
the glory of life. Appreciate
the gift of your own life.

— Donna Fargo

Most of All...
Be Happy!

Always see the goodness
in this world,
do your part in helping
those less fortunate,
walk hand in hand with
those of less talent,
follow those of more
knowledge, and
be an equal with those
who are different…

Find your special purpose
in this world full of choices
and help lead those who stray.
Become your own
individual —
set yourself apart from
those who are the same.

Most of all, be happy.
For when you are happy,
you have the key that
will open all of the world's
doors to you.

— Jackie Olson